Talking Trivia

Morgan White Jr.

Talking Trivia
© 2009 Morgan White, Jr. All Rights Reserved.

All illustrations are copyright of their respective owners, and are also reproduced here in the spirit of publicity. Whilst we have made every effort to acknowledge specific credits whenever possible, we apologize for any omissions, and will undertake every effort to make any appropriate changes in future editions of this book if necessary.

No part of this book may be reproduced in any form or by any means, electronic, mechanical, digital, photocopying or recording, except for the inclusion in a review, without permission in writing from the publisher.

Published in the USA by:
BearManor Media
P O Box 71426
Albany, Georgia 31708
www.bearmanormedia.com

ISBN 1-59393-336-3

Printed in the United States of America.

Contents

	Dedication	vii
	Foreword	xi
	Introduction	ix
1.	**Father and Son**	1
	Answers 79	
2.	**Two Letter Answers**	4
	Answers 81	
3.	**Coffee**	7
	Answers 82	
4.	**Alphabet Soup**	10
	Answers 83	
5.	**Expressions of 1 Person**	12
	Answers 84	
6.	**2 Pair of Letters**	15
	Answers 86	
7.	**The Candy Game**	18
	Answers 87	
8.	**Eyes**	21
	Answers 89	
9.	**Finish What You Start**	24
	Answers 90	
10.	**Before & After**	27
	Answers 92	
11.	**Six Education**	31

Talking Trivia

	Answers 94	
12.	**Insults**	34
	Answers 95	
13.	**State Name Fun**	37
	Answers 97	
14.	**Paper Game**	40
	Answers 98	
15.	**Stage & Screen**	43
	Answers 100	
16.	**Themes 4 You**	46
	Answers 101	
17.	**A Capital Idea**	49
	Answers 103	
18.	**What's Up Doc?**	52
	Answers 105	
19.	**2 If by Sea**	55
	Answers 106	
20.	**Reeling In The Years**	58
	Answers 108	
21.	**Just Once**	62
	Answers 109	
22.	**Triple Ripple**	65
	Answers 111	
23.	**Pop Culture Cars**	69
	Answers 113	
24.	**Just the Facts**	72
	Answers 114	
25.	**The Morgan Game**	75
	Answers 116	

As you leaf through these pages you will find a new kind of trivia. You've played games at home before, and made teams in your local pub for prizes. You've guessed while watching your favorite sports team, and argued with your friends about the right answers. You have never seen a trivia game like this before. This is not Trivial Pursuit; it is trivia perfection.

If your topic is state capitals, then you will find clues like "Homer Simpson's Boss," that leads you to Montgomery, Alabama. The things from your everyday life will send you back in time to past TV, movies, music, and even a school subject or two. You will be amazed at the unique way to reach the right answers. Guessing has never been so much fun! There's something here for everyone, but no one will know it all. Challenge yourself to see if you have what it takes to play the perfect trivia game.

Dedication

This book is dedicated to:

Terrie Zuehl, Nancy Risty and Andrew Fielding

For without their efforts this book would not have been compiled and completed by deadline.

A special thank you to Janet Novack for her cover design.

Foreword

Morgan has entertained people from coast to coast with his unique style of trivia. He has been called "The Phenomenal Master of Trivia", "The Professor of Trivia", and other exclamations. I have known Morgan for over 20 years, and I have seen him change his shows to keep them fresh for the "triviots" that have followed him for years. Triviot is one of the unique words that Morgan has created for the fans that follow him from one venue to another trying to stump him with some small bit of trivia. I am constantly amazed at the way Morgan can retrieve information so quickly. It's fun to watch him think!

You will not be able to answer all these questions; however, you will have a chance to remember the past TV shows, products, dates, and events that make up the games in this book. You might recall school lessons of geography, or even the name of your uncle's car. Morgan can and does pull all of this information out with little effort. I hope you find these games to be fun reminiscences of your childhood and perhaps you will even join the ranks of triviots.

Morgan's other unique phrase is "ticky-ticky," which is what I did to write this forward. Ticky-ticky is the sound made by striking the keys on a computer keyboard, and therefore explains your use of a computer.

I am honored to be a member of Morgan's inner circle of family, and to have the opportunity to work on this book. I've also created Morgan's website. You can ticky-ticky Morgan there; however, Morgan does NOT ticky-ticky. For Morgan, trivia is easy, technology is not!

— Terrie Zuehl Novack

Introduction

This book came about from my original trivia games played on WBZ 1030 AM in Boston. In the early 1990's, I was a guest every 3 or 4 months on the David Brudnoy Show. David and his callers loved the different games that I created on subjects like candy, State Capitals or the name, "DAVID" (a game not in this book).

Eventually I became a fill in host at 'BZ. Usually I am on air overnight, the midnight to 5 a.m. shift. The 4 a.m. hour is when I would use my new trivia games. It would be common for 40 or 50 people to call in to qualify to win the prize of the night.

The 25 games in this book reflect the best received of the hundreds of games played while on the air.

Thanks to my former and current WBZ colleagues for having me as their guest and for taking off a night or two so we could all have fun playing trivia.

The late Dr. David Brudnoy
Jordan Rich
The late Paul Sullivan
Steve LeVeille

Morgan

Father & Son
Dedicated to Evan White

*The greatest memory in my life is **not** of all the things I've done on radio or television, or my appearances on stage in Vegas; these are all just achievements. My most powerful memory is holding my newly adopted six week old son in my right hand. The power of the father and son bond is best understood by being a father or a son. I wanted to write a game that would be a tip of the hat to real and fictional fathers and sons. Thanks Evan.*

The clues lead you to a father and son.

1. NASCAR's 3 & 8 (or 88)
2. Former Haiti Rulers
3. Tweety's Nemesis and His Son
4. NBC Junkyard Kings
5. The Singing Guthries
6. Carmella's Husband and Son

2 Talking Trivia

7. Acting Douglases
8. Dear Old Dad and His Son His Son
9. They Sandwiched the Clinton Presidency
10. Betty's B Boys
11. Taylors of Mayberry
12. Boxer Father Football Son
13. Caroline's Departed Brother and Father
14. Superman the Earth Answer
15. Superman the Krypton Answer
16. *The Rifleman*
17. New York, New York
18. Wax Winged Pair
19. Enterprise Klingons
20. Munster Men
21. High Chief Peter Maivia's Son and Grandson
22. America's First Father-Son Presidents
23. They Covered "Just The Two of Us"
24. Huxtable Men
25. Cosby Men
26. Bocephus
27. Lost Clownfish Story
28. Jane's Acting Pa and Brother

29. Race Bannon Protected Them
30. NFL Griese Quarterbacks
31. *Jetson* Males
32. David Nelson's Brother and Father
33. Tough Men Tender Chicken
34. Their House Was a Museum
35. Mr. Wilson's Neighbors
36. They Were Best Friends
37. A Complex Father and Son
38. Holy Ghost
39. The Ricardos
40. Wally's Brother and Father
41. Burger King Sandwiches
42. The Force Was With Them
43. Springfield's Cop and His Kid
44. Golf Woods
45. 70's & 80's Boston Bruins
46. They're Great
47. Muppeteers
48. They Lived Long and Prospered
49. Cher's Rocker and Son
50. *The Lion King*

Two Letter Answers

For each question, find the two letter answer. The answers can be abbreviations or actual words. U.S. or us are examples of each.

1. Affirmative Answer
2. Comedy Central's First Name
3. Mr. Woolworth
4. Science Fiction Mr. Wells
5. Ready for My Close Up Mr. DeMille
6. Lower Case Mr. Cummings
7. A Bread Song
8. Stone Age Comic Strip
9. Military Trainer
10. Because of the Wonderful Things He Does
11. A Daisy Rifle's Ammo

Letter Answers   5

12. Mr. Penney's Store
13. Letters That Followed Magnum
14. Rubber Man Mr. Goodrich
15. Vehicle-to-Vehicle Voice Communicator
16. Sports Video Game
17. Chevy, Buick, Oldsmobile etc.
18. Pufnstuf
19. A Boxer's Result of His Best Punch
20. Stuart Little's and Charlotte Web's Mr. White
21. San Francisco/Philly/Dallas Mouthy Wide Receiver
22. Very Very Clear TV Reception
23. Captain's Second-in-Command
24. Michigan Frog's Network
25. Fonzie's Hairstyle
26. Former Competitor of Lowes and Home Depot
27. Your Hospital Caretaker
28. Herbie Car 53
29. Lionel Railroad Gauge
30. The Maharishi's Concept
31. Tampon Made for Women by Women
32. You Get the Maxx for the Minimum

33. In Other Words
34. Cops Holding You for Your Own Good
35. Mr. Barnum
36. NBC's Over-a-Decade-Long Prime Time Medical Series
37. Follows 2009
38. College Dorm Watchdog
39. Gym Class
40. Army Man Joe
41. Giants QB Legend Tittle
42. Owned Island Hoppers
43. Special Effects
44. A Whopper Relative
45. A Pound
46. Musically Speaking Just Add 1
47. Cleanup Hitter who Only Hits
48. Not Allowed to Play Anymore
49. Maternal Abbreviation of Bay State
50. Paternal Abbreviation of Keystone State

Coffee

The clues that follow will lead to an answer that relates to coffee.

1. Delivered Bruce Almighty Coffee
2. According to the Song-Where There is a Lot of Coffee
3. Danny Thomas's Sponsor
4. Time of A & P's Coffee
5. Home of the 14 oz Cup
6. 50/50 Additive
7. Teddy Roosevelt's Maxwell House Line
8. 60's Stewardesses Rachel Jones's & Trudy Baker's Book
9. 9 to 5'er Recess
10. Orange Rim Pot
11. Pequot Whaler

12. Alliterative Dunkin Donuts (DD) Drink
13. Classic *Airplane* Line
14. Dr. Evil's Brand
15. Canada's #1 Location
16. Better Coffee Than a Millionaire Can Buy
17. Lizzie McGuire Hangout
18. A.K.A. Joe DiMaggio
19. Coffee Siblings
20. A Word for Coffee, Cream and Sugar
21. Man's Three Letter Name for Coffee
22. *SNL* Mike Myers's Skit
23. Shot of Booze in Your Morning Brew
24. Magnolia State Community
25. Emerald Isle Beverage
26. Sugar Shack Drink
27. Just Add Hot Water
28. Small Square Pastry
29. Where the *Friends* Hang Out
30. Coffee Crystals Brand
31. Non-Dairy Creamer
32. Pam Grier 70's Black Action Film

33. DD Rebus
34. 3 Letter Coffee Vessel
35. 60's Beatnik Hangout
36. Alliterative Group of Women
37. 2004 Roberto Benigni Film
38. Fronted the *Detroit Guitar Band*
39. 4-Named Coca Cola Product
40. Summer Time Bowl and Spoon Treat
41. Mickey D's Hot Mistake
42. MSNBC A.M. News Show
43. *Guess Who* Hit
44. Snifter Beverage
45. Matriarch of The Beast's Kitchen
46. Movie *Night Shift* Money Holder
47. Mickey D's Cocaine Controversy
48. Two 60's Variety Show Hosts who Allegedly Drank Coffee During Their Monologues
49. *Bonanza* Sheriff
50. Al Hirt Instrumental

Alphabet Soup

Every response will give you the phonetics of a single letter.

1. Second Level Movies

2. The Spanish Fox's Mark

3. The Kissing Letter in a Letter

4. Scott Fitzgerald

5. Letter That Accompanies a Football Fan's Prop of a Picket Fence

6. Smallest Article of Speech

7. Rating That Should Keep Younger Teens out of a Theatre

8. Network That Gave us "Talk Soup"

9. An affirmative in the Navy

10. "____" Your Hair Smells Terrific!

11. One of Michael Corleone's Wives

12. Dorothy's Auntie

13. One of a Reporter's First Six Questions

14. Model Miss McPherson

15. That Middle Piano Key

16. Needle-Injected Street Drug

17. First Word of American Anthem

18. First Letter of all American Commercial Airliners' Serial Numbers

19. Monty Hall's Announcer Mr. Stewart

20. What Kept the Princess From Sleeping

21. A Lineup

22. A Lady Sheep

23. World's Most Consumed Beverage

24. Roadway Curve

25. 80's Science Fiction TV Series

26. The 21st Letter Twice

Expressions of 1 Person
Dedicated to Ken Meyer

Morgan & I were talking one day and spoke about various expressions that sports broadcasters used that became their slogan or trade mark. For example, Mel Allen, long time "Voice of the Yankees," would often use the phrase **"How about that!"** *after an exciting play. Legendary Red Sox announcer, Ned Martin, would use the word* **"Mercy!"** *The next game is a result of that chat.*

Each answer is the name of the person who says the clue phrase

1. Yabba Dabba Do
2. Shazam
3. Quite
4. D'oh
5. Fascinating
6. Righty-O

7. Bam
8. AAAAY
9. Jeepers
10. Whee Dogies
11. Engage
12. Work
13. Geronimo
14. Cowabunga
15. Sitzvitz
16. Caramia
17. Solid
18. ALVIN
19. Timber
20. Ka Bong
21. Hoo Rah or Oorah
22. Olympia
23. Dy-no-mite
24. Stifle
25. The A Through Z Song
26. Narf
27. Supercalifragilisticexpialidocious
28. Yes!!

29. T-t-t-h-hat's All Folks
30. Gooooooooal
31. Kimosabe
32. Fahrvergnügen
33. Bully
34. Jinkies
35. Babaloo
36. Elementary
37. Shazbot
38. Pilgrim
39. Whammy
40. Chocolate
41. Howdee! I'm so Proud to be Here!
42. Practice?????
43. Plastics
44. Fore!
45. Rosebud
46. Wowzers
47. Good Night and May God Bless
48. Say Good Night Dick
49. Mom Always Liked You Best
50. Do You Believe in Miracles?!

2 Pair of Letters

Every four letter answer will contain two pair of repeating letters.

1. Midday
2. Bird Sound
3. Chinese Food Platter
4. Sandra Bullock's Secret Sisterhood
5. *Mamma Mia* People
6. Gophers Ruffled Feather & Running Board
7. Extinct Bird
8. Grandmother
9. Mr. Ma
10. Crazy Zany Person
11. Candy Beads

12. Peter Potomus Buddy
13. To Laugh
14. Wrestler Mr. Brazil
15. A *Teletubbie* Friend
16. A *Teletubbie*
17. Singer Miss Pennison
18. Insulting T.V. Tube Slang
19. Army Slang For Scuttlebutt
20. Liz Taylor *Simpsons* Line
21. Skater Miss Starbuck
22. Head Smurf
23. Guitar Pedal
24. *Star Wars* Personnel Carrier
25. Actress Miss Neuwirth
26. Talking Doll's First Word
27. Midget Wrestler Sky
28. Hostess Snack
29. Horn Sound
30. *Godfather III*'s Joey
31. Dorothy's Dog
32. Ballet Dress

33. *Laugh-In's* Chastisement

34. Quick Draw's Louie

35. Goodbye

36. Fashion Magazine

37. Maurice Chevalier Film

38. Former Nugget Mr. Vandeweghe

39. Ex-Red Sox Center Fielder Crisp

40. Sam Giancana Nickname

41. Skunk LePew

42. An Extended Play Album or 45

43. King of Siam's Woman

44. Bart & Lisa's Bus Driver

45. Tubby's "Little" Friend

46. Contemporary Actress Miss Rogers

47. George Bailey's Daughter

48. "Oh Zephyr Winds Which Blow On High, Lift Me Now so I Can Fly."

49. Darling Julie Andrews

50. Main 9-11 Terrorist Pilot

The Candy Game

Name the candy which could have been named for . . .

1. The Reason You Work 40 Hours (or More) Each Week
2. Someone With the "Dropsies"
3. The Actress Who Starred in *Harold & Maude*
4. Fergie's Titular Jurisdiction
5. Follows $99,999.99
6. A Main New York City Thoroughfare
7. One of the First Phone Cards
8. The Ill-Fated Clown at Mary Richards TV Station
9. Piles of Dirt
10. A Spicy Mexican Dish
11. When a Celestial Body Explodes
12. Alexander Dumas Misnamed Quartet

13. John Williams's & Keith Lockhart's Favorite Kind of Music
14. Lois Lane's Coworker
15. Competition in Which you Must Traverse 137,300 Feet
16. Group of Women Named Dorothy
17. The Sound You Make When You Eat a Potato Chip
18. Phobos's and Demos's Father
19. The Word "Good" Twice
20. Richard Nixon's Secretary of State
21. A Brand of Car Stereo
22. One of Mayberry's Pyles
23. What a Kept Woman Calls Her Rich Man
24. A Term to Describe Peter Paul Rubens's Women
25. A Candy a Geologist Would Dig
26. A Physical Display of Affection
27. Edible Salems and Winstons
28. A Type of Slick Con Artist
29. A Cheerleader's Tools
30. A Rodent's Possessions
31. A Little Girl's Pair of Shoes
32. Mack the Knife

33. A Way You Affectionately End a Letter
34. Mr. Jobs's and Mr. Wozniak's Company
35. A Sarcastic Laugh
36. Orson Welles's Most Famous Movie Role
37. The ¼ Cleansing Cream Soap
38. One of the Rice Krispies Kids
39. Body Part Found at Madame Tussaud's
40. Fictional Dukakis/Eisenhower Presidential Ticket
41. Japanese WWII Fighter Plane
42. Collaboration Between 007's Boss and Dorothy's Aunt
43. Part Played by Dustin Hoffman's Actress Character
44. Teenager's Compliment for His Really Cool Father
45. Third Year Students
46. Tootsie Roll Dwarves
47. Mr. October #44
48. Homer Simpson's Candy
49. Tops the Andes, Alps and Mt. Everest
50. Very Gullible Person

Eyes

All clues point to an answer with the word "Eye" in it.

1. A Marble
2. *Rocky III*
3. Lone Star State Song
4. An Old Biblical Adage
5. Fay Dunaway Flick
6. Result of a Punch
7. Pirate Wear
8. Strong to the Finish
9. Father of Frozen Foods
10. Revolutionary War Battle Cry
11. A National Bird With Great Vision
12. Kim Carnes Hit

13. Concurring Agreement
14. Conjunctivitis
15. Begins With A Big **E**
16. Softest Body Skin
17. Daktari Big Feline
18. TV Network Icon
19. Ben Stein's Product
20. One of two of Your 32
21. Frankie Valli Carried Your Books From School Song
22. Superior Athletic Skill
23. Unkind Nickname for One Who Wears Glasses
24. Shaft, Magnum and Jim Rockford
25. B.J. Thomas Song
26. Robert Conrad & Connie Stevens Show
27. Alliterative nickname for John Havlicek
28. Macbeth Ingredient
29. The Bad in *The Good, The Bad, And The Ugly*
30. Smokey & Rick James Duet
31. Person Who Watched the Crime
32. From the Neck up Physician's Four Specialties
33. Van Morrison Hit

34. A Late Airplane Flight
35. An Enemy of Daredevil
36. Transformer Slogan
37. Describe the Purple People Eater
38. A Liquor Drink that Shocks You
39. Magician's Credo
40. Crystal Gayle
41. Bobby Vee Song
42. Jealousy
43. Sugarloaf
44. Almost A Photo Finish
45. Dromedary Based Adage
46. Define Beauty
47. Casino Camera Above Security
48. 2 Ones in Dice
49. An *Entertainment Tonight, Extra* Info. Show
50. Connie Chung Mid-90's TV Series

Finish What You Start

Every answer begins and ends with "M".

1. Borax's 20
2. Down By the Old
3. Melts in Your Mouth, Not in Your Hand
4. Interoffice Communication
5. Felix Unger's Girlfriend
6. Maternally Named Flower
7. Ol' e-i-e-i-o's Place
8. Dedication to the Dearly Departed
9. The Kid In The Middle
10. A Clairvoyant
11. Hawaiian PI
12. A Thousand Years

13. Sidney Biddle Barrows or Heidi Fleiss
14. A 60's Men's Deodorant
15. Gaining Speed Downhill
16. A Vegas Casino & A Film Company
17. Martin Lawrence's Type of Security
18. Where Paintings Live
19. Computer Equipment
20. Wreaking Havoc
21. Koran Followers
22. Socialist Philosophy
23. Wanting to Own More and More Things
24. Norm Crosby Verbal Fault
25. To Purposely Hurt
26. Your Female Teacher
27. Above Grant's Tomb
28. Lowest Price Charged
29. Halfway Through the Course Exam
30. The Late Mr. Begin
31. Fungi
32. Sought After Spy Photographic Dot
33. Polarity

34. Luna Light
35. Office Correspondence Area
36. Meow Entertainment
37. 1900
38. At Home Michael Keaton
39. Played Perry Mason in the 70's
40. Dogpatch's J.P.
41. They Sang Pop Music
42. Pine Tree State Web Address
43. Where Mickey & Tinkerbell Live
44. Richie and Joanie's Mother
45. Magic Emporium Toy Store Owner Dustin Hoffman
46. Gotham's Arkham
47. 21st Century Men's Magazine
48. A Soldier's Duds
49. Bionic Man's Limb
50. Shakespeare's Puck's Play

Before & After

I did this game in the mid 90's on the David Brudnoy Talk Show heard Monday through Friday evenings on WBZ Radio Boston, and approximately two years later this style of game appeared on "Wheel of Fortune". Coincidence? I will leave this up to the reader to decide.

Two clues will lead to two answers that are meant to overlap/merge.

1. A *Beatles* Song About a Sexagenarian / A Scandalized 50's Game Show

2. Ludwig's Classic Symphony / Marilyn McCoo and Billy Davis Jr.'s Group

3. Woolworth's / Agatha Christie's Classic Murder Who Done It

4. Dimensions of a Sheet of Typing Paper / Standard East Coast Late News Time

5. A Juice with Kale, Celery and Other Vegetables / T.V. Show About the Bradford Brood

6. Measurements of a Glossy Photo / Battle of Hastings Year

7. A Radio Operator's Acknowledgement / A Vehicle For Rough Terrain

8. A 60's Insect Repellant / Classic Yuletide Song

9. Peter Gent Satire About Football / Football Speed Measurement

10. A Nickname for the Continental United States / Nick Nolte, Eddie Murphy Movie

11. McGarrett TV Show / Levi's Pants

12. Zager and Evans Song / Edwin Starr's Song

13. Our Second War with England / Classic Film About Men on a Jury

14. Barbara Feldon's Spy Character / Beginning Point of a "Brewsky" Song

15. Celebratory Athletic Hand Gesture / Jack Nicholson Early Film Hit

16. U.S Independence Year / *Music Man* Song

17. Karen Valentine TV Show / Slang for 25 Cents

18. James Bond / A Convenience Store

19. Number of Blackbirds Baked in a Pie / ABC News Show

20. Where You Can Get Your Kicks / Lee Majors Bionic Character

21. An Equitable Split / Paul Simon's Method for Dumping a Partner

22. Spielberg "Bomb" About WWII / Bonnie Franklin TV Series

23. Chuck Berry's Song About a Teenager / Pirate Song

24. Yul Brynner, Steve McQueen and Company / The 'Un-Cola'

25. The First Year of the Carter Administration / A "Kookie" TV Show

26. The World's Greatest Comic Magazine / First Line of the Gettysburg Address

27. Marlon, Jermaine, Jackie, Tito, Michael / Minute Maid Juice Product

28. Len Barry's Biggest Hit / A Defunct PBS Kids Show

29. JFK's Boat / Morris's Cat Food

30. U.S. Bomber Plane First Built in the 50's / A Card Game Learned the Hard Way

31. Rat Pack Film About the Cavalry / Robert Redford Spy Film

32. A Complete Rotation / Where You Would See Andy Rooney

33. Bradbury's Book Burning Book / An Elvis Movie and Song

34. A Baby's Bad Age / Old Saying About One too Many People

35. *Top Gun* Jet / Columbus's Big Year

36. The Third *Airport* Movie / Snow White's Friends

37. Fox Show About a Quintet of Siblings / The T.V. & Movie Phone Exchange

38. The Day of Infamy / 3 Musketeers Credo

39. New Years Day / Movie About a Woman Supreme Court Justice

40. Traditional Columbus Day / Johnny Mathis Will Love How Long?

41. Replaced Pierce Brosnan as Bond / Sitcom Coach

42. Super Freak / Spock's Captain

43. Gambling's 21 / TV's *24*

44. Kermit's Theme Song / Peter Parker's Enemy in the First *Spiderman* Movie

45. Redundant Directional Finder / Played a TV P.I.

46. He Sang "I'm Too Sexy for My Shirt" / Yabba Dabba Dude

47. Vietnam Era Defoliant / Powdered Beverage That Went to the Moon

48. Lindsay Lohan, Tina Fey Movie / Cyndi Lauper Breakthrough Hit

49. Prince's Drummer / U.S. Great Seal Latin Phrase

50. Calvin Broadus / Hot July and August Temperatures

Six Education

Each clue leads you to an answer with "6" in it.

1. Troy Donahue's Houseboat
2. Battle of Hastings
3. 60's Spy Toy
4. Todd & Buzz Road
5. Will Smith & Stockard Channing
6. Revolutionary Musical
7. *Motley Crüe* Guy
8. Damien Number
9. Steve Austin
10. Doris Day & Brian Keith
11. Ford & Heche
12. Dudley Moore Movie

13. Throw Overboard
14. 4 & 20 Blackbirds
15. Beer, Soda, or Abs
16. Normal Body Temp
17. Sam Colt's Peacemaker
18. The Prisoner
19. Maxwell Smart
20. UK Secret Intelligence Service
21. April O'Neil Employer
22. An Engine
23. The Pilgrim Pope
24. Haley Joel Osment Flick
25. *? & the Mysterians*
26. NBA Best Player Off The Bench Award
27. Amusement Park
28. A 3 + 3 Roll of the Dice
29. Tom Clancy Novel
30. Precedes Bond
31. 1967 Middle East Battle
32. A Yard
33. Funeral Parlor HBO Series

34. Git Fiddle
35. They "Leave a Light on for You"
36. Jan, Cindy, Marcia, Bobby, Peter, Greg
37. Casino Apparatus
38. When God Created Man
39. 1800 Hours
40. Follows 5 Golden Rings
41. *NY Post* Gossip Location
42. Scoring a SS Error
43. Bill Cosby Box Office Bomb
44. Same Thing Either Way
45. Potentate Tongue Twister
46. Mound to Plate
47. 60's Insect Repellant
48. *Chicago* Song
49. Sam Spade or Dick Tracy Sign Off
50. NHL Elite

Insults

The clues below tell you who is insulting and being insulted. The answer is the insult.

1. Fred to Lamont
2. Archie to Mike
3. Burkhalter to Klink
4. The Great Gazoo to Fred & Barney
5. Oliver to Arnold
6. Daffy to Bugs
7. Moe to Larry
8. Ali to Foreman
9. Eddie to Beaver
10. Hawkeye to Frank (FF)
11. Archie to Edith

12. Dr. Smith To The Robot (BB)
13. Agnew Triple N's to the Press
14. Bad Guys to Lucas McCain
15. Penguin to Henchmen
16. Mr. Magoo to Other Drivers
17. The Neighborhood to Charlie Brown
18. Mrs. Chatsworth Osborne Sr. to Maynard
19. George Jefferson to Tom and Helen Willis
20. Fred Blassie to Enemies
21. Townspeople to Cher
22. Villain to Scooby's Gang
23. Ralph to Ed
24. Bob to Doug McKenzie
25. The *Talk Soup* Crew To John Henson
26. Vinnie to Mr. Kotter
27. Wilona to Bookman
28. 70's & 80's Fans to the New Orleans Saints Team
29. Don Rickles to Everyone
30. Fans to Bobby Heenan
31. Potsie to Ralph
32. 40's to 60's Hood to NY Beat Cop

33. Red Sox Fans to Dick Radatz
34. Hippie to a Policeman
35. McCoy to Spock
36. Mel to Vera
37. Buchanan High to Kotter's Class
38. Joan Rivers to Heidi Abramowitz
39. Kids to TRIX Rabbit
40. Yosemite Sam to Bugs
41. Friends to Warren Weber
42. Sgt. Belker to Criminal
43. Al Bundy to Marcy
44. Aykroyd to Curtin in the "Point-Counterpoint" Skit
45. Wayne Arnold to Brother Kevin
46. Klingon to a Non-Klingon
47. Lou Costello to Himself
48. Laverne to Shirley and Back
49. *Friends* About Their Neighbor
50. Top Cat to Officer Dibble

State Name Fun

Here's a place where geography is fun! Every clue leads you to an answer with the name of a state in it.

1. She Covers Your Pancakes
2. 60's Bee Gees Song
3. Mamas & Papas Round Song
4. 3 "W's"
5. Billy Joel Classic
6. JJ's Mom's Full Name
7. Rhyming Drink
8. Bless Your Pea Picking Heart
9. Where It's a Treat To Beat Your Feet
10. Music Man City & State Song
11. John Wayne and Gold Fever

12. Robert Conrad's First TV Series
13. A Mark Twain Book
14. 3-0 Super Bowl Quarterback
15. Peter Fonda & Brooke Shields Film
16. A Type of Chicken
17. Unforgettable Ship Slogan
18. Musical Perry Como Question
19. Country Line Dance
20. Famous Musical
21. Only Great Lake Entirely in the U.S.
22. TV Theme Line About *Real McCoys* Origin
23. Carry Me Back
24. Frankie Valli & The 4 Seasons
25. *Designing Women*'s Theme
26. Ron Guidry's Nickname
27. 70's R&B Group Sang "Roller Coaster For Your Love"
28. 3M Company
29. Covered North America For Over 1 Million Years
30. The Gem State
31. Where Washington, Lincoln, Jefferson & Teddy Roosevelt Live

32. Andy & Barney's Home Town & State
33. Beverage in the Tall Can
34. Coors Brewery Home
35. Jack Nicholson & Marlon Brando Film
36. Coen Brothers' Film
37. Dennis Weaver As A Vet
38. Normandy Beaches
39. Marshal Sam McCloud's Hometown
40. Land Of Lincoln State
41. Not Reading Or Shortline
42. Path Named for the Place Between California and Washington
43. Where Cat Ballou Was To Be Hanged
44. First State To Secede From The Union
45. Governor Bill Clinton's State
46. Sang "Carry On My Wayward Son"
47. Third Triple Crown Location
48. The First Primary (Not A Primary)
49. Rob Lowe & Jodie Foster Film
50. Brendan Fraser's Movie Pitcher

Paper Game

These clues lead to an answer with the word paper in it. Even with computers, all paper will not disappear.

1. Owned Puff
2. Delivers Your *New York Times*
3. George Plimpton's Sports Book
4. Presses Down on Your Desk Stuff
5. Dionne Warwick 60's Hit
6. Bronson is a Mafia Man
7. Sticky Insect Catcher
8. An Official Introspective Document
9. Preceded Xerox Copying
10. PH for You
11. Write With & Write On

12. Circular File Waste Container

13. Charmin

14. Rosie

15. Should Begin A Meal On Your Lap

16. Ron Howard Directing Michael Keaton

17. Real Estate Final Step

18. Daniel Ellsberg

19. Zig Zag

20. Where Trees Get Converted To Reams

21. It May Take on Water

22. Leaving Receipts, You Criminal

23. Harmless Ferocious Feline

24. A Marie Osmond Hit

25. Don't Paint in the Room, Use

26. I'm As Busy As A One-Armed

27. A Box Of 5000 Sheets

28. 8 1/2 X 14 Legal

29. Magician's Flaming Prop

30. Hardly Any Width

31. Non-Notarized Will

32. Kindergarten Kids Cut it Up

33. Wraps Food
34. A Supermarket Checker's Two Options To You
35. One From a Ream of 500
36. A Mills Brothers Hit
37. A Type Of Parchment
38. Imitate a WWII German Checkpoint Guard
39. *USA TODAY*
40. A Pen With A Heart Logo
41. Small Slips
42. Make It. Fly It.
43. Professor Kingsfield
44. A Stationery Chain
45. Kodak
46. Kleenex
47. Goes With A Picnic For Your Food
48. A Child's Game's 3 Options
49. A Flower
50. Envelops Gifts

Stage & Screen
Dedicated to Jason Roberts

I have challenged Morgan with new ideas for games and rules that go with them. I took special interest in the idea of a stage and screen game since theater is a passion of mine and together we "Ticky-Tickied" this game. "Ticky-ticky" is Morgan's phrase to describe anything done on a computer.

Each single word clue will lead you to the name of a musical which has been both a stage production and a motion picture.

1. Tomorrow
2. Excalibur
3. Follicles
4. Stampede
5. Nightclub
6. Fortune Teller

7. Merry-Go-Round
8. Tulsa
9. $500,000
10. Mask
11. Aquanet
12. Rumble
13. Birdcage
14. Plant
15. Lube
16. Tradition
17. Argentina
18. Polynesia
19. Windmills
20. Etcetera
21. Gamblers
22. Illinois
23. Kids
24. Edelweiss
25. Trombones
26. Pygmalion
27. Auntie
28. Crucifixion

29. Flop
30. Dogpatch
31. Widget
32. Teapot
33. Crocodile
34. Motor Car
35. Summertime
36. People
37. Pinball
38. One
39. Transsexual
40. Pickpockets
41. Rome
42. Twister
43. Landlord
44. Flappers
45. Forefathers
46. Baseball
47. Avenue
48. Bull's-eye
49. Chinatown
50. Loincloth

Themes 4 You

These clues are themes of a person or T.V. show. The answers are that person or show.

1. Riverboat Ring Your Bell
2. Made the Hit Parade
3. Or Even Your Year
4. Ya'll Come Back Now
5. Tease Him A Lot
6. He Sleeps 'Til Noon
7. Piece of the Pie
8. Hers and Hers Alone
9. A Hero who Sneezed
10. Turn the World On
11. They're All Together Ooky

12. And Life is Heaven
13. Ready and You're Willing
14. You Take the Bad
15. Are You Ready Kids?
16. We're too Busy Singin'
17. Who Believes in Doing Good and Doing Right
18. Adventures Waiting Just Ahead
19. Roamed Through the West
20. Including a Private Eye
21. Seen a Twister Mister
22. Sweeping the Clouds Away
23. You are my Wife
24. Keep Them Dogies Movin'
25. Not a Single Luxury
26. Been Waiting for You
27. Never Meaning no Harm
28. I'm Walking on Air
29. Been Seen With Farrah
30. Takes Everything You've Got
31. Thank You For Being a Friend
32. Read us Any Rule

33. *Of a Lovely Lady*
34. *Your Head Above Water*
35. *Our Music Could Pay*
36. *Rolling Down the Tracks*
37. *Won't You Try Him*
38. *Head of the Clan*
39. *In a Savage Land*
40. *Anything From a Pussycat*
41. *So Shiny and New*
42. *What a Crazy Pair*
43. *Make it on Time*
44. *Talking Man-to-Man*
45. *Cuz Life's Too Short*
46. *Whatever Became of Me?*
47. *We're a Happy Family*
48. *Darling Help Me Understand*
49. *Ask the Local Gentry*
50. *Situation Well in Hand*

A Capital Idea

Every answer will make you think of a United States capital. No comments on the bad puns.

1. Legendary 70's Steelers Running Back Who Wore Number 32
2. WWII Battle Ship Attack Cry
3. T.V. Show About "Moving on Up"
4. A Wild West Taming Firearm
5. Jimmy Stewart Film About a Desert Plane Crash
6. A Cake With Custard Filling and Chocolate Frosting
7. Famous 1600 New England Court Cases
8. Departed King of Late Night T.V. Talk Show Host
9. Lee Majors 6 Million Dollar Man Character
10. Homer Simpson's Boss
11. Stag Icon for an Insurance Company

12. "Surrey with the Fringe on Top" Musical
13. Mountainous British Landmark
14. A Means of Administering to a Boil
15. Mr. October Reggie
16. Warner Brothers' Cowboy
17. Felix Unger's Roommate
18. 1987 *Moonstruck* Oscar Winning Actress
19. A Smack It, Crack It, Candy Bar
20. JFK Press Secretary
21. German Beer Brand Fraulein
22. *Lovin' Spoonful* Hit "Feline" Song
23. Cigarette or Bicycle
24. Foresight or Divine Direction
25. A Type of Grape
26. Black Cast Member of *The Mod Squad*
27. The Capital Phonetically Hidden Within Another Capital
28. The Man Who Succeeded Julius Caesar
29. Another Name for Oscar Meyer Wieners
30. An 80's Potato Snack With a Name That Sounded Like an Interjection

31. Now Retired Former NHL Boston, Washington, Phoenix, Buffalo, Ottawa, Montreal Player
32. Vice Presidential Song
33. Writer of *The Goonies*
34. Former WWE Star A.K.A. The Brahma Bull
35. A Christian Rite
36. George Burns *Oh God!* Costar
37. To Revere "To Sir With Love" Singer
38. Oscar Nominee of *The Wings of the Dove*
39. Freddy Cannon's Rhyming Titled Song
40. Legendary Celtic Stop Sign
41. If Miss Dunaway Became Father Christmas
42. One Hundred Percent Rabbit
43. Kujo's Owners
44. The Lost Continent
45. Yearly Memorial Day Sporting Event
46. What a French Chef Might Call His Potato Skinner
47. Not Poor Man, not Beggar Man, Not Thief
48. Othello's Wife
49. 1964 Peter Ustinov Movie Filmed in Istanbul
50. A Horse's Saline Lollypop

What's Up Doc?

Every clue leads you to the name of a real or fictional doctor.

1. Bond's 1st Enemy
2. Dr. Gillespie's Protégé
3. Pimp Dan Aykroyd
4. Danced to "Lara's Theme"
5. *Motley Crüe* Song
6. A Medicine Woman
7. Non-Worrying Bomb Lover
8. Your Baby and You
9. Horton, Lorax and Who's
10. Samantha & Endora's Physician
11. Bette Midler's Dentist

What's Up Doc? 53

12. Enterprise's Sickbay Surgeon
13. Animal Talker
14. Philly's Basketball 76ers
15. Mystical Magical Marvel's Character
16. *Sports Illustrated* Football Picker
17. Benton Quest's Rival
18. Trapdoor PJ's
19. Mr. Hyde's Buddy
20. Snoop Dogg's Buddy
21. He Was in the Right Place but it Must Have Been the Wrong Time
22. Marty McFly's Mentor
23. Jupiter 2 Bad Guy
24. Detroit's Mercy Killing Physician
25. Mini Me's Mentor
26. Tardis
27. Oprah Protégé
28. Ms. Schlessinger
29. Animated Professional Therapist
30. "Good Sex"
31. Rob Lowe's Failed Series

32. 10-2-4 Beverage
33. Mad Music Crazy Comedy
34. Igor's Master
35. *Fantastic 4* Enemy
36. Jack Klugman Character
37. *Rolling Stone* Cover Boy
38. Lost in Africa
39. His Dream Still Lives
40. Trapper John, Hawkeye & B.J.'s Whipping Boy
41. Nazi "Angel of Death"
42. Surgeon for First Heart Transplant
43. *Coma* Physician
44. 1 of Snow White's Dwarves
45. Spiderman's Arch Enemy
46. ABC-TV Network Medical Spokesperson
47. 80's Fireballing Mets Pitcher
48. Johnny Carson's *Tonight Show* Band Leader
49. Reagan's Bearded Surgeon General
50. Famous TV Psychologist/Writer

2 If by Sea

These clues will lead you to answer with the name of a famous sailing vessel. We gave you a bonus one.

1. Palindromic Paddler
2. Shirley Temple's Ship
3. Columbus's Ship
4. Green Bottled Scotch
5. The Love Boat
6. "My Heart Will Go On" Ship
7. Quentin McHale's Boat
8. Japanese Battle Ship circa. 1930
9. Thor Heyerdahl's Ship
10. Capt. Crunch's Ship
11. Gilligan and the Skipper's Craft

12. Harry Orwell Boat
13. Sub Built by Admiral Nelson
14. Tom Clancy's Russian Sub
15. Bad Guys' Home in Water World
16. Takes Passenger Around Niagara Falls
17. The Presidential Yacht
18. Johnny Horton's Song
19. Fletcher Christian's Transportation
20. "Call Me Ishmael"
21. Ship in *Beanie & Cecil* Show
22. Brought King Kong to NY
23. Dartmouth, Eleanor, The Beaver
24. Camelot's Aircraft Carrier
25. Troy Donahue's TV Houseboat
26. Gilbert & Sullivan's Musical Ship
27. Tony Soprano's Cabin Cruiser
28. Shuttle Star Ship/Aircraft Carrier
29. Battling Civil War Ironclad
30. 2 Ships That Crashed Off Cape Cod in 1956
31. Grandfather & Me's Sloop
32. Great Lake Tanker Disaster

33. Darwin's "Dog"
34. John Denver's Cousteau Tribute
35. Hydrofoil Yacht in *Thunderball*
36. Covered Wagon Nautical Nickname
37. Humphrey and Kate's Boat
38. Ship They Want Remembered
39. Where the *Beatles* Lived
40. Most Popular Private Boat Name
41. Shelley Winters Ocean Liner Disaster Film
42. Capt. Nemo's Sub
43. Jason's Vessel
44. Pearl Harbor Memorial
45. Raymond Burr in a Wheelchair
46. Historic Mississippi River Landmark
47. Jack Sparrow Ship
48. Where the PLO took Leon Klinghoffer
49. Spielberg's Slave Revolt Ship
50. Capt. Cook's Ship
51. Ship that Failed in its Attempt to Sink Old Ironsides

Reeling in the Years
Dedicated to Generosa Aiello

"Generosa is on the line" WBZ listeners would be told, and all knew the game was over and a winner would be chosen. Generosa gave Morgan the idea for the next game with the explanation, *"I am 96 years old [born in MA in 1912] and there are many things I have wanted to ask, so many things I wanted to know through the years, I figured a game about years would be just the thing."*

Here is a game where all the answers are years, for *the Princess of Peabody*.

1. Spielberg WWII "Bomb"
2. Big Brother Year
3. *Space Odyssey* Sequel
4. Revolutionary Musical
5. Columbus Sailing The Ocean Blue

Reeling in the Years

6. Words on *Wizard of Oz*'s Balloon
7. Liz Damon *Orient Express* Hit Song
8. Raquel Welch in a "Fur Bikini"
9. The Song "Simple" *Simon Says* Performers
10. Magna Carta
11. Martin Landau Sci Fi Series
12. Futuristic Zager & Evans Song
13. *Star Trek: First Contact* Year
14. Date the UN Created the State of Israel
15. Billy Crystal Directed Baseball Movie
16. "Oh What A Night" Next Line
17. Battle of Hastings
18. Plymouth Rock
19. "A Certain Smile" Film
20. "A Certain Smile" Movie Sequel
21. Red Sox's "Impossible Dream" Year
22. Legendary Maine to New York Blizzard
23. Sutter Mill Year
24. Battle of New Orleans: Twice
25. Black Sox
26. Final *Airport* Sequel

27. Black Tuesday
28. The Day The Music Died
29. Frye & Lila Year (*Futurama*)
30. Upscale Jose Cuervo Tequila
31. Teenaged Tom Brady's Favorite Team
32. The Day of Infamy
33. First year of Prohibition
34. There was U2, Madonna, etc.
35. Bob Hope Film That Introduced "Thanks For The Memories"
36. Last Year of Prohibition
37. Fisk Waving the Ball Fair
38. Either Year of the New York World's Fair
39. *Duck Dodgers* Year
40. President Kennedy Assassination Date
41. World Trade Center Destruction
42. Super Bowl's XX Year
43. D-Day
44. *My Mother The Car* Year and Model
45. *Time* Magazine's "Man of the Year" First Year

46. Modern Baseball Era Year with No World Series
47. 007 Movie Debut Year
48. Bobby Orr "Flying Past the Goal" Year
49. Freddie Prinze's Car
50. Group That Covered "Fool on the Hill"

Just Once

These are quotes heard <u>ONLY ONCE</u> on a T.V. series. The show's name is the answer.

1. Hello, Ball

2. The New Alante

3. It is Ballooooon!

4. It Means, The Cattle are Dying

5. Master of my Domain

6. I was Wrrrrr---I was Wrrrrr--I was Wrrrrrong"

7. Citizen's Arrest!

8. Eep Op Orp Ah Ah

9. You Know What Happens When you Assume

10. Listen to the Mockingbird POW

11. Vitameatavegamin

12. I Saw it in the Window and Just Couldn't Resist It
13. Mooshi Mooshi
14. Oh My Nose
15. As God is my Witness I Thought Turkeys Could Fly
16. My Name is Talking Tina and I am Going to Kill You
17. How Long is This Story? I'm 80 I Have to Plan.
18. Shame, Come Back Shame
19. Niagara Falls
20. . . . . Where There'll be No Tribble at All
21. There are No Ribs Like Adams Ribs
22. He Stirs His Tea Anti-Clockwise
23. It's a Floor Wax, It's a Dessert Topping
24. Bingo Bango Bongo and Irving
25. Moo Goo Gai Pan
26. Uhni Ufts
27. And **That** was the Night the Lights Went Out in Georgia
28. Put Your Foot up on the Lady's Thumb
29. Odela Kawasaki. Odeka Kawasaki
30. Cops! He yelled, Cops!
31. Crush! Kill! Destroy!
32. Ever Feel Like the World is a Tuxedo and You're a Pair of Brown Shoes?

33. I Brought You into This World and I can Take You Out
34. Shotzi Toy Company
35. Ivan, Did you see the Sun Rise This Morning?
36. No Comment Until the Time Limit is Up.
37. Get This Bucket Movin'
38. Spy Girl
39. Mermaid, Mermaid in the Sea Will You Grant a Wish for Me?
40. This is a Defunct Parrot
41. Have you Been Sending Money Home to your Mother's Again?
42. I Want my Daddy's Records
43. Gum Will be Perfection
44. If You are Gonna Have a Change of Life You Gotta do it Right Now
45. This is why Some Animals Eat Their Young
46. When the Apocalypse Comes, Beep Me.
47. How Come we Overcame and Nobody Told Me?
48. It's a Dog Eat Dog World and I'm Wearing Milkbone Underwear
49. I Love You Like the Mother I had Committed Against her Will
50. All Alone-All Alone-All Alone-All Alone, God is Everywhere-Everywhere- Everywhere-Everywhere

Triple Ripple

This set of three clues will lead to answers that will have three segments: The first is a single letter answer, the second is two words beginning with the same single letter, and the third is three words beginning with that same letter.

1.   Nickname of a Men's Christian Association
   2. Kid's Toy
   3. Stevie Wonder's Love Song

2.   The Sex Vitamin
   2. He Played a CA Motorcycle Cop
   3. King of Siam's Favorite Phrase

3.   Political 60's Film
   2. Ben Vereen's Kid Show
   3. The Mazda Tribute's Three Favorite Words

4.   Letter on Shirley's Roommate's Blouses
   2. Nickname of a NY Statue
   3. Superman's Three Loves

5. Kind of Man J. Edgar Was
   2. 50's and 60's Lonesome Comic
   3. Ruffled Feather & Running Board

6. Randolph Scott's Tall Movie
   2. That Cratchit Kid
   3. Mr. Allen's *Home Improvement* Character

7. *Mad Mad Mad Mad World*'s Big Money Location
   2. Prior to 2004, Name Who Was President When the Red Sox Last Won the World Series
   3. Fozzie Bear's Signature Greeting

8. The Round Fat Battery
   2. Luke and Bo's Female Cousin
   3. What Mutley Was to His Owner

9. Square Hopping Bert
   2. Questioning Literary Abbreviation
   3. 60's Feuding Cereals and Their Company

10. First Person Singular
    2. Hoosier State and Capital
    3. Three O' Clock in Italy

11. Inferior Brand
    2. Mexican Beer
    3. Grannie's Moonshine

12. 3.0 Grade
    2. 30's Cartoon Sex Symbol
    3. A Citizen's Watchdog Agency

13. Orange Juice Vitamin
    2. The Little Tramp
    3. Ohio's Three Largest Cities

14. Das Boot
    2. Fruit of the Loom's Super Hero Briefs
    3. Robert Hall Fought Prices Going There

15. The Roman Numeral for Five
    2. Julie Andrew's in Double Drag
    3. I Came . . . and So On

16. Basketball Shot
    2. Frank's Train Robbing Brother
    3. Spiderman's Boss

17. "Butterfly" on Broadway
    2. A Cat's Cat
    3. How Much Heart Joe Hardy Had

18. Circle's Convenience Store
    2. Played President Dave
    3. Striking Out The Side

19. A Camera Stop
    2. He Played Gleason's "Crazy" Friend
    3. *Laugh-In* Award

20. A Steering Wheel Column's First Letter
    2. Mr. Maravich's Nickname
    3. Boxing Nickname of Dick Van Dyke's Character

21. President Truman's Middle Initial
    2. 60's Kids T.V. Host
    3. The Grinch in Three Words

22. The Smallest Article
    2. Mr. Steffi Graf
    3. Road Rescuers

23. 60's Black Activist Rap Brown
    2. Played TV's Dr. Johnny Fever
    3. Minnesota Twins Domed Home Field

24. Ampersand Substitute
    2. Peter Pan's Home
    3. Musical That Cost Boston the Babe

25. Challenger's Failed Rings
    2. Those Who Are Licensed to Kill
    3. *Marvel* Comics Deranged Doctor

26. Follows PG-13
    2. Played "That Cat Shaft"
    3. Original Three School Subjects

Pop Culture Cars

As you drive, pay attention to the vehicles around you. Each pop culture clue and auto maker will lead you to the model of a vehicle as an answer.

1. Mel Gibson Film & A 70's Ford
2. *Star Trek* Series & Soccer Mom Van
3. 60's Futuristic Cartoon Dog & Chevy Van
4. A Reindeer & Volkswagen
5. Original American Gladiator & A Saab
6. Heart Song & 60's AMC Car
7. *Popeye*'s Pet & Army Vehicle
8. Spartan's Film & Reborn Chrysler
9. Little Anthony's Guys & A Chrysler
10. John Wayne and Robert Mitchum Film & A Cadillac
11. *Addams Family* Member & 70's Volkswagen

12. Horse TV Show & A Plymouth
13. Industrial Spy Doris Day & A 60's Chevy
14. Cosby's Miss Bledsoe & A 60's Pontiac
15. Andrew Dice Clay Film & Henry's Alliterative Vehicle
16. *Speed Racer*'s Car & A Lincoln Mercury Mach
17. Sang "Native New Yorker" & Honda Van
18. Keanu Reeves Trilogy & Toyota Van
19. Disney's Hannah & A Current Pontiac
20. Clint Walker Western & A Type of Jeep
21. Johnny Yuma & A Honda
22. Immortal Sean Connery & Toyota Van
23. Steve Wynn's Former Strip Hotel & A Mitsubishi
24. Selleck as a PI & 70's Dodge
25. *Full House* Dog & A 60's Mercury
26. Andrew Duggan Western & A Mitsubishi
27. Cowboy Ty Hardin & A Ford Truck
28. Charles Addams' Magazine & A 60's Chrysler
29. Sexy Over 30's Woman & 60's/70's Mercury
30. Bird Man's Bird & A Current Dodge
31. Racing James Garner & A 60's Pontiac
32. Beep Beep, Beep Beep & A Plymouth

Pop Culture Cars

33. Don't Feed After Midnight & A 70's AMC
34. The Fresh Prince's Neighborhood & A 50's/60's Chevy
35. All of Us & A 60's Rambler
36. Deion Sanders' Nickname & A Dodge
37. Daredevil's Girl & A Classic Buick
38. X-Men Woman & A Nissan
39. Pina Colada Song a.k.a. & A Current Ford
40. Lance Burton's Hotel Home & A Classic Chevy
41. 1950's Vegas Strip Casino & A Legendary Buick
42. Billy Zane's Super Hero Flick & A Classic Rolls Royce
43. *101 Dalmatians'* Cruella & A Classic Caddy
44. Jack Webb's Production Company & A 70's Continential
45. America's First Nuclear Submarine & A 50's/60's Dodge
46. Riviera Country & A 60's Dodge
47. Rosemary Clooney's Commercial Product & A 50's Dodge
48. Warren Beatty & Diane Keaton Film & A Plymouth Van
49. Old W.C.W. Wrestling Show & A Dodge Van
50. Jim Carrey's Ace & A 70's Pontiac

Just the Facts

These clues will make you think of the names of cops for your answer.

1. Captain of the Old One-Two
2. Top Cat's Cop
3. Just One More Question
4. David Starsky's Partner
5. Arnold the Teacher
6. Mary Beth Lacey's Partner
7. Cop Acronym
8. Mack Sennett's Guys
9. Wowsers
10. Spenser's Buddy
11. Rockford's Guy
12. He Bat-Signals Batman

13. Francis Muldoon's Partner
14. Badge 714
15. Make His Day
16. Pete, Linc, and Julie
17. Loved His Lolly Pop
18. Danny Williams's Boss
19. Who Breathless Mahoney Loved
20. Neighborhood Watch Cop
21. *Barney Miller* Spin Off
22. Jets and Sharks Foil
23. *Adam 12* Occupants
24. Superman's Buddy
25. Marshall Sam McCloud's Chum
26. Chased Richard Kimble
27. Wheelchair-Bound Policeman Chief Robert
28. He Swatted Criminals
29. Cop in a Rolls
30. Howard Rollins and Sidney Poitier
31. Citizen's Arrest
32. Played by George Kennedy
33. Shatner on Earth

34. Rock Hudson With or Without a Wife
35. Oscar's and Felix's Friend
36. Late *Law & Order* Cop
37. Nob Hill Lt.
38. Big Screen/Little Screen Leslie Nielson Lt.
39. Pacino Playing NY Honest Cop
40. Don't Do the Crime
41. *Police Woman*
42. Pizza Man
43. Bare Butt Dennis Franz
44. Mechanical Peter Weller
45. OJ Trial Fibber
46. Vampire Cop
47. Peter Gunn Inside Guy
48. Former Ram Plays a T.V. Cop
49. Smothers Brothers Peace Officer
50. *Hong Kong Phooey* Switch Board Operator

The Morgan Game
Dedicated to Rob Brooks

We've had every other game in this book, and now it's time for Morgan. In the past, he has written games using WBZ personalities names, and now it is time for his. As producer on the overnight shift, Rob has heard more of these games than just about anyone, so when he asked to have a Morgan game, it seemed the right thing to do. As a tip of the hat to Rob, the WBZ listening audience, and triviots everywhere, I hope you enjoy! By the way triviot is Morgan's affectionate term for anyone who knows and loves trivia.

Every answer will contain "Morgan" in some way.

1. Played Izzie's fiance, Denny, on *Grey's Anatomy*
2. Massachusetts Quadruped
3. TV Cop George Kennedy
4. Pete of *Pete and Gladys*
5. Investment Firm

6. Cutthroat Geena Davis
7. 70's & 80's Patriots & Eagles Wide Receiver
8. Old Navy Spokesperson
9. Clark Kent's Galaxy Boss
10. Bespectacled 60's Game Show Panelist
11. Ribald Gong Show Judge
12. 21st Century Houston Astros 3rd Baseman
13. Hand Built Since 1910
14. VERY, Very Top Heavy Legendary Ex-Stripper
15. Haystacks Calhoun's Hometown
16. Danger Island's Two Heroes
17. Sunday Comic Doctor
18. *Boy Meets World* Kid Sister
19. Current L.P.G.A. Athlete
20. ESPN Sunday Night Baseball Broadcaster
21. James, Warren and Virgil's Two Other Brothers
22. P.G.A. Senior Circuit Pro
23. Manager of the Red Sox in the 80's
24. Parrot Bay's Maker
25. Town & Country on the Right Bank of The Murray River

26. Sang "'Til A Tear Becomes A Rose" with Keith Whitley
27. 21st Century USA Female Gymnast
28. 21st Century USA Male Gymnast
29. God to Evan and Bruce
30. Famous in Monterey, California
31. Movie Production Company
32. HBO Sex Hostess
33. King Arthur's Enemy
34. "Somewhere Over The Rainbow" Wizard
35. David Warner & Vanessa Redgrave Film
36. The Kissing Bandit
37. A Treasurer under FDR
38. Played Cool Hand Luke's Boss Man
39. Start Your Day
40. 19th Century Millionaire
41. Andrea Doria Famous Survivor
42. Ann Blyth Movie
43. Keystone State Locale
44. *Bananas in Pajamas'* Three Girls
45. Who Shot Bobby
46. Mid-1880's to Early-1900's Money

47. Muddy Water's Real Name
48. Mary Richards's Best Friend
49. *Saturday Night Live* Alum circa. Mid 90's-2003
50. Swashbuckler Steve Reeves Early 60's Movie

Answers

Father & Son

1. Dale Earnhart & Dale Earnhart Jr.
2. Baby & Papa Doc
3. Sylvester & Sylvester Jr.
4. Sanford & Son
5. Arlo & Woody
6. Anthony & Anthony Jr.
7. Kirk & Michael
8. Auggie Doggie & Doggie Daddy
9. The Bushes
10. Barney & Bam Bam
11. Andy & Opie
12. Ken Norton Jr & Sr.
13. John Kennedy Jr. & Sr.
14. Clark & Jonathan
15. Jor-El & Kal-El
16. Lucas & Mark
17. Frank Sinatra & Frank Sinatra Jr.
18. Daedalus & Icarus
19. Worf & Alexander
20. Herman & Eddie
21. Rocky Johnson & The Rock

22. John Adams & John Quincy Adams
23. Will Smith & Trey
24. Cliff & Theo
25. Bill & Ennis
26. Hank Williams Jr & Sr
27. Nemo & Marlin
28. Henry & Peter Fonda
29. Jonny Quest & Dr. Benton Quest
30. Bob & Brian
31. George & Elroy
32. Ricky & Ozzie
33. Frank & Jim Purdue
34. Gomez & Pugsley
35. Dennis & Henry
36. Tom & Eddie
37. Oedipus & Laius
38. God & Jesus
39. Ricky & Little Ricky
40. Beaver & Ward
41. Whopper & Whopper Jr.
42. Anakin & Luke
43. Clancy & Ralph
44. Eldrick & Earl
45. Ken Hodge & Ken Hodge Jr.
46. Tony & Tony Jr.
47. Jim & Brian Henson
48. Sarek & Spock
49. Greg Allman & Elijah Blue
50. Simba & Mufasa

Letter Answers

1. OK
2. HA
3. F. W.
4. H. G.
5. C. B.
6. e. e.
7. If
8. B. C.
9. D. I.
10. OZ
11. BB
12. J. C.
13. P. I.
14. B. F.
15. CB
16. EA
17. GM
18. H. R.
19. KO
20. E. B.
21. T. O.
22. HD
23. XO
24. WB
25. DA
26. HQ
27. RN or MD
28. VW
29. HO
30. TM
31. OB
32. T. J.
33. i.e.
34. PC
35. P. T.
36. ER
37. AD
38. RA
39. PE
40. G. I.
41. Y. A.
42. T. C.
43. CG
44. BK
45. LB
46. VH
47. DH
48. DQ
49. MA
50. PA

Coffee

1. Juan Valdez
2. Brazil
3. Sanka
4. 8 O'Clock
5. Mel's Diner
6. Half and Half
7. "Good to the Last Drop"
8. "Coffee, Tea, or Me"
9. Coffee Break
10. Decaf
11. Starbuck
12. Coffee Coolata
13. "I take my coffee black like my men."
14. Seattle's Best
15. Tim Horton
16. Chock Full O' Nuts
17. Digital Bean
18. Mr. Coffee
19. Hills Brothers
20. Regular
21. Joe
22. Coffee Talk
23. Coffee Knock
24. Hot Coffee, N.M.
25. Irish Coffee
26. Espresso Coffee
27. Instant Coffee
28. Coffee Cake
29. Central Perk
30. Folgers
31. Coffee Mate
32. Coffy
33. America Runs on Dunkin
34. Mug or Cup
35. Coffee House
36. Coffee Klatch
37. Coffee & Cigarettes
38. Dennis Coffy

Answers

Alphabet Soup

39.	Caffeine-Free Diet Coke	1.	B
40.	Coffee Ice Cream	2.	Z (Zorro)
41.	Coffee Lid Lawsuit	3.	X
42.	Cup of Joe	4.	F.
43.	No Sugar Tonight In My Coffee	5.	D
		6.	A
44.	Coffee Brandy	7.	R
45.	Mrs. Potts	8.	E
46.	Coffee Can	9.	I (aye)
47.	Coffee Stir Story	10.	G
48.	Dean Martin & Jackie Gleason	11.	K
		12.	M (Em)
49.	Roy Coffee	13.	Y (Why?)
50.	Java	14.	L (Elle)
		15.	C
		16.	H (heroin)
		17.	O
		18.	N
		19.	J
		20.	P

Expressions of 1 Person

21. Q (Queue)
22. U (ewe)
23. T
24. S
25. V
26. W

1. Fred Flintstone
2. Gomer Pyle
3. Commander McBragg
4. Homer Simpson
5. Spock
6. Felix The Cat
7. Emril
8. Fonzie
9. Dennis the Menace
10. Jed Clampett
11. Capt. Picard
12. Maynard G. Krebs
13. Paratrooper
14. Ninja Turtles
15. David The Gnome
16. Gomez
17. Linc Hayes
18. David Seville
19. Lumberjack
20. Quick Draw

Answers

21. Marines
22. Hercules
23. JJ
24. Archie Bunker
25. Big Bird
26. Pinky
27. Mary Poppins
28. Marv Albert
29. Dennis the Menace
30. Pablo Ramirez
31. Tonto
32. VW
33. Teddy Roosevelt
34. Velma
35. Ricky Ricardo
36. Sherlock Holmes
37. Mork
38. John Wayne
39. Peter Tomarken
40. Farfel
41. Minnie Pearl
42. Allen Iverson
43. William Daniels
44. Golfers
45. Charles Foster Kane
46. Inspector Gadget
47. Red Skelton
48. Dan Rowan
49. Tom Smothers
50. Al Michaels

2 Pairs of Letters

1. Noon
2. Peep
3. Pu Pu
4. Ya Ya
5. ABBA
6. GoGo
7. Dodo
8. Nana
9. Yo-Yo
10. Kook
11. Ju Ju
12. So So
13. Ha Ha
14. Bobo
15. Nu Nu
16. LaLa
17. Cece
18. Boob
19. Poop
20. Da Da
21. Jo Jo
22. Pa Pa
23. Wa Wa
24. AT AT
25. Bebe
26. Ma Ma
27. Lo Lo
28. Ho Ho
29. Toot
30. Za Za
31. Toto
32. Tu Tu
33. No No
34. Baba
35. Ta Ta
36. Elle
37. Gigi
38. Kiki

Answers   *87*

The Candy Game

39.	Coco	1.	Payday
40.	Momo	2.	Butterfinger
41.	Pepe	3.	Baby Ruth
42.	Eppe	4.	York Peppermint Patty
43.	Anna	5.	100 Grand bar
44.	Otto	6.	Fifth Avenue
45.	Lulu	7.	Spree
46.	Mimi	8.	Chuckles
47.	Zuzu	9.	Mounds
48.	Isis	10.	Hot Tamales
49.	Lili	11.	Starburst
50.	Atta	12.	Three Musketeers
		13.	Symphony
		14.	Clark
		15.	Marathon
		16.	Dots
		17.	Crunch
		18.	Mars
		19.	Bon Bons

20. Oh, Henry
21. Alpine
22. Goobers
23. Sugar Daddy
24. Chunky
25. Rock Candy
26. Kisses or Hugs
27. Candy Cigarettes
28. Smoothie
29. Pom Poms
30. Squirrel Nuts
31. Mary Janes
32. Heath
33. Forever Yours
34. Candy Apple
35. Snickers
36. Candy "Kane"
37. Dove
38. Crackle
39. Wax Lips
40. Mike & Ike
41. Zero
42. M&M
43. Tootsie Roll
44. Pop Rocks
45. Junior Mints
46. Midgets
47. The Reggie Bar
48. Butterfinger B B's
49. Snow Caps
50. Sucker

Eyes

1. Cat's Eye
2. "Eye Of The Tiger"
3. "Eyes of Texas"
4. An Eye For An Eye
5. *Eyes of Laura Mars*
6. A Black Eye
7. Eye Patch
8. Popeye
9. Clarence Birdseye
10. Don't Shoot 'Til You See The Whites of Their Eyes
11. Eagle Eye
12. "Bette Davis Eyes"
13. Eye To Eye
14. Pink Eye
15. Eye Chart
16. Eye Lid
17. Clarence The Cross-Eyed Lion
18. CBS Eye
19. Clear Eyes
20. Eye Teeth
21. "My Eyes Adored You"
22. Hand-Eye Coordination
23. 4 Eyes
24. Private Eye
25. "The Eyes of A New York Woman"
26. *Hawaiian Eye*
27. Bouncing Buckeye
28. Eye of Newt
29. Angel Eyes
30. Ebony Eyes
31. Eyewitness
32. Eyes, Ears, Nose and Throat
33. Brown Eyed Girl
34. Red Eye
35. Bullseye
36. More than meets the eye

37. 1-Eyed 1-Horned Flying…
38. Eye Opener
39. The Hand is Quicker Than The Eye
40. "Don't It Make My Brown Eyes Blue"
41. "The Night has 1,000 Eyes"
42. Green Eyed Monster
43. "Green Eyed Lady"
44. Eyelash
45. Easier for a Camel to get Through the Eye of a Needle
46. Eye of the Beholder
47. Eye in the Sky
48. Snake Eyes
49. Eye on Hollywood
50. Eye to Eye

Finish What You Start

1. Mule Team
2. Mill Stream
3. M&M
4. Memorandum
5. Miriam
6. Mum
7. MacDonald's Farm
8. Memoriam
9. Malcolm
10. Medium
11. Magnum
12. Millennium
13. Madam
14. Mitchum
15. Momentum
16. MGM
17. Maximum
18. Museum
19. Modem
20. Mayhem

Answers

21. Muslim
22. Marxism
23. Materialism
24. Malapropism
25. Maim
26. Marm
27. Mausoleum
28. Minimum
29. Midterm
30. Menachem
31. Mushroom
32. Microfilm
33. Magnetism
34. Moonbeam
35. Mailroom
36. MTM
37. MCM
38. Mr. Mom
39. Monty Markham
40. Marryin' Sam
41. M
42. Maine.com
43. Magic Kingdom
44. Marian Cunningham
45. Mr. Magorium
46. Mental Asylum
47. Maxim
48. Military Uniform
49. Mechanical Arm
50. Midsummer Night's Dream

Before and After

1. "When I am **64**" **Thousand Dollar Question**
2. Beethoven's **Fifth Dimension**
3. 5 and "**10 Little Indians**"
4. 8 ½ X **11 P.M.**
5. V**8** *is Enough*
6. 8 X **1066**
7. 10 **4 Wheel Drive**
8. 6 "**12 Days of Christmas**"
9. North Dallas **40 Yard Dash**
10. Lower **48 Hours**
11. *Hawaii* **5 0 1**'s
12. *In the Year 25***25 Miles to Go**
13. War of 18**12 Angry Men**
14. Agent "**99 Bottles of Beer on the Wall**"
15. High **5 Easy Pieces**
16. 17 "**76 Trombones**"
17. *Room 222* **Bits**
18. 007 **11**
19. 4 and **20-20**
20. "Route **66**" *Million Dollar Man*
21. 50-"**50 Ways to Leave Your Lover**"
22. 194**1 Day At A Time**
23. Sweet Little **16 Men on a Dead Man's Chest**
24. *The Magnificent* **7**-UP
25. 19**77 Sunset Strip**
26. Fantastic **Four Score and Seven Years Ago**
27. *The Jackson* **5 Alive**
28. One Two **Three Two One Contact**
29. PT 109 **Lives**
30. B-**52 Pickup**

Answers

31. Sergeants **Three Days of the Condor**
32. **3**60 Minutes
33. *Fahrenheit 45***1 Night With You**
34. The Terrible **Two's Company Three's a Crowd**
35. F-**1492**
36. Airport 77 **Dwarves**
37. *Party of* **555**
38. December 7, 194 **1 For All, All For One**
39. January **First Monday in October**
40. October **"12 of Never"**
41. Daniel **Craig T Nelson**
42. Rick **James T. Kirk**
43. Black **Jack Bauer**
44. "It's Not Easy Being **Green" Goblin**
45. Tom **Tom Selleck**
46. Right Said **Fred Flintstone**
47. Agent **Orange Flavored Tang**
48. *Mean* **"Girls Just Want to Have Fun"**
49. Sheila **e pluribus unum**
50. Snoop **Dog(g) Days of Summer**

Six Education

1. Surfside 6
2. 1066
3. Sixth Finger
4. Route 66
5. 6 Degrees of Separation
6. 1776
7. Nikki Sixx
8. 666
9. *Million Dollar Man*
10. *With 6 You Get Eggroll*
11. *6 Days 7 Nights*
12. *6 Weeks*
13. Deep 6
14. 6 Pence
15. 6-Pack
16. 98.6
17. 6 Shooter
18. #6
19. Agent 86
20. MI-6
21. Channel 6
22. Slant 6 or V-6
23. Pope Paul VI
24. 6th Sense
25. 96 Tears
26. 6th Man Award
27. 6 Flags
28. Hard 6
29. Rainbow 6
30. 006
31. 6 Day War
32. 36 Inches
33. 6 Feet Under
34. 6 String Guitar
35. Motel 6
36. Brady 6
37. Big 6
38. Day 6
39. 6 p.m.
40. 6 Geese a-Laying

Insults

41.	Page 6	1.	Big Dummy
42.	E-6	2.	Meathead
43.	Leonard Part 6	3.	Idiot
44.	6 of 1, A Half Dozen of the Other	4.	Dum Dums
		5.	Stupid Pig
45.	The Sixth Sheiks 6th Sheep is Sick . . .	6.	You're Despicable
		7.	Porcupine
46.	60 Feet 6 Inches	8.	Mummy
47.	6-12	9.	Squirt
48.	25 or 6 to 4	10.	Ferret Face
49.	6, 2 & Even	11.	Dingbat
50.	Original 6	12.	Bubbleheaded Boobie
		13.	Nattering Nabobs of Negativism
		14.	Sodbuster
		15.	Fine Feathered Finks
		16.	Road Hogs
		17.	Blockhead
		18.	You Nasty Boy
		19.	The Zebras

20. Pencil Neck Geek
21. Half Breed
22. Meddling Kids
23. You are a Mental Case
24. Hoser
25. Skunk Boy
26. Up your Nose with a Rubber Hose
27. Buffalo Butt
28. The Aints
29. Hockey Puck
30. Weasel
31. Sit On It
32. Flat Foot
33. Monster of the Bullpen (With Affection)
34. Fuzz/Pig
35. You Cold Blooded...
36. Dingy
37. Sweat Hogs
38. Tramp
39. Silly Rabbit Trix are for Kids
40. Varmint
41. Potsie
42. Dogbreath/Hairball
43. Chicken...
44. Jane, You Ignorant Slut
45. Butthead
46. Patak
47. I'm a Bad Boy
48. Shlemiel, Shlimazl
49. Ugly Naked Guy
50. Why Officer Dribble

State Name Fun

1. Vermont Maid
2. "Massachusetts"
3. "California Dreamin'"
4. Walla Walla, Washington
5. NY State of Mind
6. Florida Evans
7. Alabama Slama
8. Tennessee Ernie Ford
9. In the Mississippi Mud
10. Gary, Indiana
11. North To Alaska
12. *Hawaiian Eye*
13. Connecticut Yankee In King Arthur's Court
14. Joe Montana
15. "Wanda Nevada"
16. Rhode Island Red
17. Remember The Maine
18. What Did Delaware?
19. Texas 2 Step
20. *Oklahoma*
21. Lake Michigan
22. "From West Virginny They Came to Stay in Sunny Californiay"
23. To Old Virginny
24. *The Jersey Boys*
25. "Georgia On My Mind"
26. Louisiana Lightning
27. Ohio Players
28. Minnesota Mining & Manufacturing
29. Wisconsin Glacier
30. Idaho
31. Mt. Rushmore, South Dakota
32. Mayberry, N.C.
33. Arizona Ice Tea
34. Golden, Colorado
35. Missouri Breaks
36. *Fargo*, North Dakota

Paper Game

37. Kentucky Jones
38. Omaha Gold Utah Sword Juneau
39. Taos, New Mexico
40. Illinois
41. Pennsylvania Railroad
42. Oregon Trail
43. Wolf City, Wyoming
44. South Carolina
45. Arkansas
46. Kansas
47. Belmont Park, Maryland
48. Iowa Caucus
49. Hotel New Hampshire
50. Steve Nebraska

1. Jackie Paper
2. Paper Boy
3. *Paper Lion*
4. Paperweight
5. Paper Mache
6. *Valachi Papers*
7. Fly Paper
8. White Paper
9. Carbon Paper
10. Litmus Paper
11. Pen & Paper
12. Paper Basket
13. Toilet Paper
14. Paper Towel
15. Paper Napkin
16. The Paper
17. Passing Papers
18. Pentagon Papers
19. Rolling Papers
20. Paper Mill

Answers

21. Paper Boat
22. Paper Trail
23. Paper Tiger
24. "Paper Roses"
25. Wall Paper
26. Paper Hanger
27. A Carton Of Paper
28. Pad of Paper
29. Flash Paper
30. Paper Thin
31. Not Worth The Paper It's Printed On
32. Construction Paper
33. Wax Paper
34. Paper or Plastic?
35. A Sheet of Paper
36. "Paper Doll"
37. Rice Paper
38. "Let Me See Your Papers"
39. Newspaper
40. Paper Mate
41. Note Paper
42. Paper Airplane
43. *Paper Chase*
44. Paper Store
45. Photo Paper
46. Tissue Paper
47. Paper Plate
48. Rock, Paper, Scissors
49. Paper White
50. Wrapping Paper

Stage & Screen

1. Annie
2. Camelot
3. Hair
4. Lion King
5. Cabaret
6. Gypsy
7. Carousel
8. Oklahoma
9. Hello Dolly
10. Phantom of the Opera
11. Hairspray
12. West Side Story
13. La Cage Aux Folles
14. Little Shop of Horrors
15. Grease
16. Fiddler on the Roof
17. Evita
18. South Pacific
19. Man of La Mancha
20. The King and I
21. Guys and Dolls
22. Chicago
23. Bye Bye Birdie
24. Sound of Music
25. Music Man
26. My Fair Lady
27. Mame
28. Jesus Christ Superstar
29. The Producers
30. Li'l Abner
31. How To Succeed In Business
32. Beauty and The Beast
33. Peter Pan
34. Chitty Chitty Bang Bang
35. Porgy and Bess
36. Funny Girl
37. Tommy
38. A Chorus Line
39. Rocky Horror Picture Show

Themes 4 You

40. Oliver
41. Funny Thing Happened on the Way to the Forum
42. The Wizard of Oz/ The Wiz
43. Rent
44. Thoroughly Modern Millie
45. 1776
46. Damn Yankees!
47. 42nd Street
48. Annie Get Your Gun
49. Flower Drum Song
50. Tarzan

1. Maverick
2. All in the Family
3. Friends
4. Beverly Hillbillies
5. Welcome Back, Kotter
6. Yogi Bear
7. Jeffersons
8. Dobie Gillis
9. F-Troop
10. Mary Tyler Moore
11. The Addams Family
12. I Love Lucy
13. Scooby Doo
14. Facts of Life
15. Spongebob Square Pants
16. The Monkees
17. Kimba The White Lion
18. Speed Racer
19. Rebel
20. 77 Sunset Strip

21. *Bronco*
22. *Sesame Street*
23. *Green Acres*
24. *Rawhide*
25. *Gilligan's Island*
26. *Three's Company*
27. *Dukes of Hazzard*
28. *Greatest American Hero*
29. *Fall Guy*
30. *Cheers*
31. *Golden Girls*
32. *Laverne & Shirley*
33. *Brady Bunch*
34. *Good Times*
35. *Partridge Family*
36. *Petticoat Junction*
37. *Magilla Gorilla*
38. *Real McCoys*
39. *Have Gun Will Travel*
40. *My Mother the Car*
41. *Love Boat*
42. *Patty Duke*
43. *Saved by the Bell*
44. *The Courtship of Eddie's Father*
45. *Alice*
46. *WKRP*
47. *Barney*
48. *Mad About You*
49. *Married With Children*
50. *Mighty Mouse*

A Capital Idea

1. Frank O. Harris (Harrisburg, PA)
2. "Sink the Bismarck" (Bismarck, ND)
3. *The Jeffersons* (Jefferson City, MO)
4. The Springfield Rifle (Springfield, IL)
5. *Flight of the Phoenix* (Phoenix, AZ)
6. Boston Cream Pie (Boston, MA)
7. Salem Witch Trials (Salem, OR)
8. Johnny Carson (Carson City, NV)
9. Colonel Steve Austin (Austin, TX)
10. Montgomery Burns (Montgomery, AL)
11. The Hartford (Hartford, CT)
12. Musical *Oklahoma* (Oklahoma City, OK)
13. The White Cliffs of Dover (Dover, DE)
14. Lancing it (Lansing, MI)
15. Jackson (Jackson, MS)
16. Mr. Cheyenne Bowdie (Cheyenne, WY)
17. Oscar Madison (Madison, WI)
18. Olympia Dukakis (Olympia, WA)
19. Charleston Chew (Charleston, WV)
20. Pierre Salinger (Pierre, SD)
21. St. Paulie Girl (St. Paul, MN)
22. *Nashville Cats* (Nashville, TN)
23. Raleigh (Raleigh, NC)
24. Providence (Providence, RI)

25. Concord (Concord, NH)
26. Lincoln Hayes (Lincoln, NE)
27. Indianapolis (Annapolis, MD)
28. Augustus (Augusta, ME)
29. Frankfurter (Frankfort, KY)
30. O'Boise (Boise, ID)
31. Juneau (sounds like Juneau, AK)
32. Hail Columbia (Columbia, SC)
33. Chris Columbus (Columbus, OH)
34. The Rock (Little Rock, AR)
35. A Sacrament (Sacramento, CA)
36. John Denver (Denver, CO)
37. To Honor Lulu (Honolulu, HA)
38. Helena Bonham Carter (Helena, MT)
39. Tallahassee Lassie (Tallahassee, FL)
40. Arnold "Red" Auerbach (Baton Rouge, LA)
41. Santa Faye (Santa Fe, NM)
42. All Bunny (Albany, NY)
43. The Trentons (Trenton, NJ)
44. Atlantis (Atlanta, GA)
45. The Indianapolis 500 (Indianapolis, IN)
46. Mon Peeler (Montpelier, VT)
47. Rich Man (Richmond, VA)
48. Desdemona (Des Moines, IA)
49. Topkapi (Topeka, KS)
50. Salt Lick (Salt Lake City, UT)

What's Up Doc?

1. Dr. No
2. Dr. Kildare
3. Dr. Detroit
4. Dr. Zhivago
5. Dr. Feelgood
6. Dr. Quinn
7. Dr. Strangelove
8. Dr. Spock
9. Dr. Seuss
10. Dr. Bombay
11. Dr. Long John
12. Dr. McCoy
13. Dr. Dolittle
14. Dr. J
15. Dr. Strange
16. Dr. Z
17. Dr. Zin
18. Dr. Dentons
19. Dr. Jekyll
20. Dr. Dre
21. Dr. John
22. Dr. Brown
23. Dr. Smith
24. Dr. Kevorkian
25. Dr. Evil
26. Dr. Who
27. Dr. Phil
28. Dr. Laura
29. Dr. Katz
30. Dr. Ruth
31. Dr. Vegas
32. Dr. Pepper
33. Dr. Demento
34. Dr. Frankenstein
35. Dr. Doom
36. Dr. Quincy
37. Dr. Hook
38. Dr. Livingston
39. Dr. Martin Luther King, Jr.

40.	Dr. Frank Burns		

2 If by Sea

40.	Dr. Frank Burns	1.	Kayak
41.	Dr. Mengele	2.	Lollypop
42.	Dr. Christiaan Barnard	3.	Santa Maria
43.	Dr. Robin Cook	4.	Cutty Sark
44.	Doc	5.	Pacific Princess
45.	Doc Ock	6.	Titanic
46.	Dr. Timothy Johnson	7.	PT73
47.	Doc Gooden	8.	Yamato
48.	Doc Severinsen	9.	Kon Tiki
49.	Dr. C. Everett Koop	10.	Guppy
50.	Dr. Joyce Brothers	11.	Minnow
		12.	The Answer
		13.	Seaview
		14.	Red October
		15.	Exxon Valdez
		16.	Maid of the Mist
		17.	Sequoia
		18.	Sink the Bismark
		19.	Bounty
		20.	Pequod

Answers

21. Leakin' Lena
22. Venture
23. Boston Tea Party
24. JFK
25. Surf Side 6
26. HMS Pinafore
27. Stugots
28. Enterprise
29. Monitor or Merrimac
30. Stockholm & Andrea Doria
31. John B.
32. Edmund Fitzgerald
33. Beagle
34. Calypso
35. Disco Volante
36. Prairie Schooner
37. African Queen
38. The Maine
39. Yellow Submarine
40. Happy Hour
41. *Poseidon Adventure*
42. Nautilus
43. Argo
44. Arizona
45. Ironside
46. Delta Queen
47. The Black Pearl
48. Achille Lauro
49. Amistad
50. Endeavor
51. HMS Guerriere

Talking Trivia

Reeling in the Years

1. 1941
2. 1984
3. 2010
4. 1776
5. 1492
6. Omaha State Fair 1903
7. 1900 Yesterday
8. 1 Million BC
9. 1910 Fruit Gum Co.
10. 1215
11. Space 1999
12. "In the Year 2525"
13. 2063
14. May 14, 1948
15. "61*"
16. Late December Back in '63
17. 1066
18. 1620
19. *Summer of '42*
20. *Class of '44*
21. 1967
22. 1978
23. 1849
24. War of 1812
25. 1919
26. *The Concorde… Airport '79*
27. 1929
28. Feb. 3, 1959
29. 3000
30. 1800
31. 49ers
32. Dec. 7, 1941
33. 1919
34. 1985
35. *Big Broadcast of 1938*
36. 1933
37. 1975
38. 1939 or 1964/65

Answers

Just Once

39.	2350 (24 ½ century)	1.	*The Honeymooners*
40.	November 22, 1963	2.	*Married... With Children*
41.	September 11, 2001	3.	*F-Troop*
42.	1986	4.	*Welcome Back Kotter*
43.	June 6, 1944	5.	*Seinfeld*
44.	1928 Porter	6.	*Happy Days*
45.	1927 Charles Lindbergh	7.	*The Andy Griffith Show*
46.	1994 (due to strike)	8.	*The Jetsons*
47.	1962	9.	*The Odd Couple*
48.	1970	10.	*The Flintstones*
49.	58 Chevy	11.	*I Love Lucy*
50.	Sergio Mendes & Brasil '66	12.	*The Carol Burnett Show*
		13.	*Barney Miller*
		14.	*The Brady Bunch*
		15.	*WKRP In Cincinnati*
		16.	*The Twilight Zone*
		17.	*The Golden Girls*
		18.	*Batman*
		19.	*Three Stooges*

20. *Star Trek*
21. *M*A*S*H*
22. *The Avengers*
23. *Saturday Night Live*
24. *Gilligan's Island*
25. *The Bob Newhart Show*
26. *The Dick Van Dyke Show*
27. *Designing Women*
28. *Leave It To Beaver*
29. *The Mary Tyler Moore Show*
30. *Car 54, Where Are You?*
31. *Lost In Space*
32. *George Gobel on The Tonight Show*
33. *The Cosby Show*
34. *Hogan's Heroes*
35. *Magnum P.I.*
36. *The Adventures of Superman*
37. *Jonny Quest*
38. *Monty Python's Flying Circus*
39. *Mad About You*
40. *Rocky and Bullwinkle*
41. *Sgt. Bilko*
42. *Sanford and Son*
43. *Friends*
44. *All in the Family*
45. *Roseanne*
46. *Buffy The Vampire Slayer*
47. *The Jeffersons*
48. *Cheers*
49. *Will and Grace*
50. *Davey and Goliath*

Triple Ripple

1. Y
   2. Yo Yo
   3. Yester-me Yester-you Yesterday

2. E
   2. Eric Estrada
   3. Etcetera etc. etc.

3. Z
   2. *Zoobilee Zoo*
   3. Zoom Zoom Zoom

4. L
   2. Lady Liberty
   3. Lois (Lane) Lana (Lang) Lori (Lemaris)

5. G
   2. George Gobel
   3. Go-Go Gophers

6. T
   2. Tiny Tim
   3. Tim (the) Toolman Taylor

7. W
   2. Woodrow Wilson
   3. Wakka Wakka Wakka

8. D
   2. Daisy Duke
   3. Dick Dastardly's Dog

9. Q
   2. QQ
   3. Quaker's Quisp and Quake

10. I
    2. Indianapolis, Indiana
    3. III

11. X
    2. Dos Equis (XX)
    3. XXX

12. B
    2. *Betty Boop*
    3. Better Business Bureau

13. C
    2. Charlie Chaplin
    3. Columbus, Cleveland, Cincinnati

14. U
    2. Underoos Underwear
    3. Up, Up, Up

15. V
    2. Victor, Victoria
    3. Veni, Vedi, Vici
16. J
    2. Jesse James
    3. J. Jonah Jameson
17. M
    2. Mr. Mistoffelees
    3. Miles and Miles and Miles
18. K
    2. Kevin Kline
    3. KKK
19. F
    2. Frankie Fontaine
    3. (Flying) Fickle Finger of Fate
20. P
    2. Pistol Pete
    3. Pitter Patter Petrie
21. S
    2. Soupy Sales
    3. Stink, Stank, Stunk
22. A
    2. Andre Agassi
    3. American Automobile Association
23. H
    2. Howard Hesseman
    3. Hubert H. Humphrey
24. N
    2. Never Never Land
    3. No, No, Nanette
25. O
    2. OO (Double o)
    3. Otto Octavius Octopus
26. R
    2. Richard Roundtree
    3. 'readin, 'ritin, & rithmetic

Pop Culture Cars

1. Maverick
2. Voyager
3. Astro
4. Dasher
5. Turbo
6. Barracuda
7. Jeep
8. 300
9. Imperial
10. El Dorado
11. Thing
12. Fury
13. Caprice
14. Tempest
15. Ford Fairlane
16. Mark-5 (Lincoln)
17. Odyssey
18. Matrix
19. Montana
20. Cheyenne
21. Rebel
22. Highlander
23. Mirage
24. Magnum
25. Comet
26. Lancer
27. Bronco
28. New Yorker
29. Cougar
30. Avenger
31. Grand Prix
32. Road Runner
33. Gremlin
34. Bel Air
35. American
36. Neon
37. Electra
38. Rogue
39. Escape
40. Monte Carlo

Just the Facts

41.	Riveria		1.	*Barney Miller*
42.	Phantom		2.	Officer Dibble
43.	De Ville (Caddy)		3.	Lt. Columbo
44.	Mark 7		4.	Ken Hutchinson
45.	Polaris		5.	*Kindergarten Cop*
46.	Monaco		6.	Christine Cagney
47.	Coronet		7.	Constable on Patrol
48.	Town and Country		8.	*Keystone Kops*
49.	Nitro		9.	*Inspector Gadget*
50.	Ventura		10.	Lt. Marty Quirk
			11.	Dennis Becker
			12.	Commissioner Gordon
			13.	Gunther Toody
			14.	Joe Friday
			15.	*Dirty Harry*
			16.	Mod Squad
			17.	*Kojak*
			18.	Steve McGarrett
			19.	*Dick Tracy*
			20.	Officer Friendly

Answers

21. *FISH*
22. Officer Krupke
23. Reed and Malloy
24. Inspector Hendersen
25. Sgt. Joe Broadhurst
26. Lt. Gerard
27. *Ironside*
28. Lt. Dan Hondo Harrelson
29. Amos Burke
30. Virgil Tibbs
31. Barney Fife
32. Blue Knight
33. T.J. Hooker
34. Chief McMillan
35. Murray the Cop
36. Lenny Briscoe
37. Mike Stone
38. Frank Drebin
39. *Serpico*
40. *Baretta*
41. Pepper Anderson
42. Frank Furillo
43. Andy Sipowicz
44. Robo Cop
45. Mark Fuhrman
46. Nick Knight
47. Lt. Jacoby
48. Rick Hunter
49. Office Judy
50. Rosemary

The Morgan Game

1. Jeffrey Dean Morgan
2. Morgan Horse
3. Bumper Morgan
4. Harry Morgan
5. Morgan Stanley
6. Captain Morgan
7. Stanley Morgan
8. Morgan Fairchild
9. Morgan Edge
10. Henry Morgan
11. Jaye P. Morgan
12. Morgan Ensberg
13. Morgan Roadster
14. Chesty Morgan
15. Morgan's Corner, Arkansas
16. Chongo and Morgan
17. *Rex Morgan M.D.*
18. Morgan Matthews
19. Morgan Pressel
20. Joe Morgan
21. Wyatt and Morgan Earp
22. Dr. Gil Morgan
23. Joe Morgan
24. Captain Morgan
25. Morgan, South Australia
26. Lorrie Morgan
27. Morgan White
28. Morgan Hamm
29. Morgan Freeman
30. Morgan Winery
31. Morgan Creek
32. Katie Morgan
33. Morgan Le Fey
34. Frank Morgan
35. *Morgan*
36. Morganna
37. Henry Morgenthau Jr.
38. Morgan Woodward

Answers

39. Güten Morgen

40. John Pierpont Morgan

41. Linda Morgan

42. The Helen Morgan Story

43. Morgantown, PA

44. Morgan, Lulu and Amy

45. Morgan Brittany (Katherine)

46. Morgan Silver Dollar

47. McKinley Morganfield

48. Rhoda Morgenstern

49. Tracy Morgan

50. Morgan The Pirate

Morgan White, Jr. lives in Newton, MA.
If you'd like more information about Morgan,
contact him through his website.
www.morganwhitejr.com
or email terrie@triviamorganwhitejr.com
Just remember Morgan does not ticky-ticky,
so all messages will be passed on to him.

www.ingramcontent.com/pod-product-compliance
Lightning Source LLC
Chambersburg PA
CBHW070923160426
43193CB00011B/1559